ISBN 0 86163 023 8
© AWARD PUBLICATIONS LIMITED 1980.
1st FLOOR, GOODYEAR HOUSE,
52-56 OSNABURGH STREET,
LONDON NW1 3NS.
REPRINTED 1993.

PRINTED IN BELGIUM.

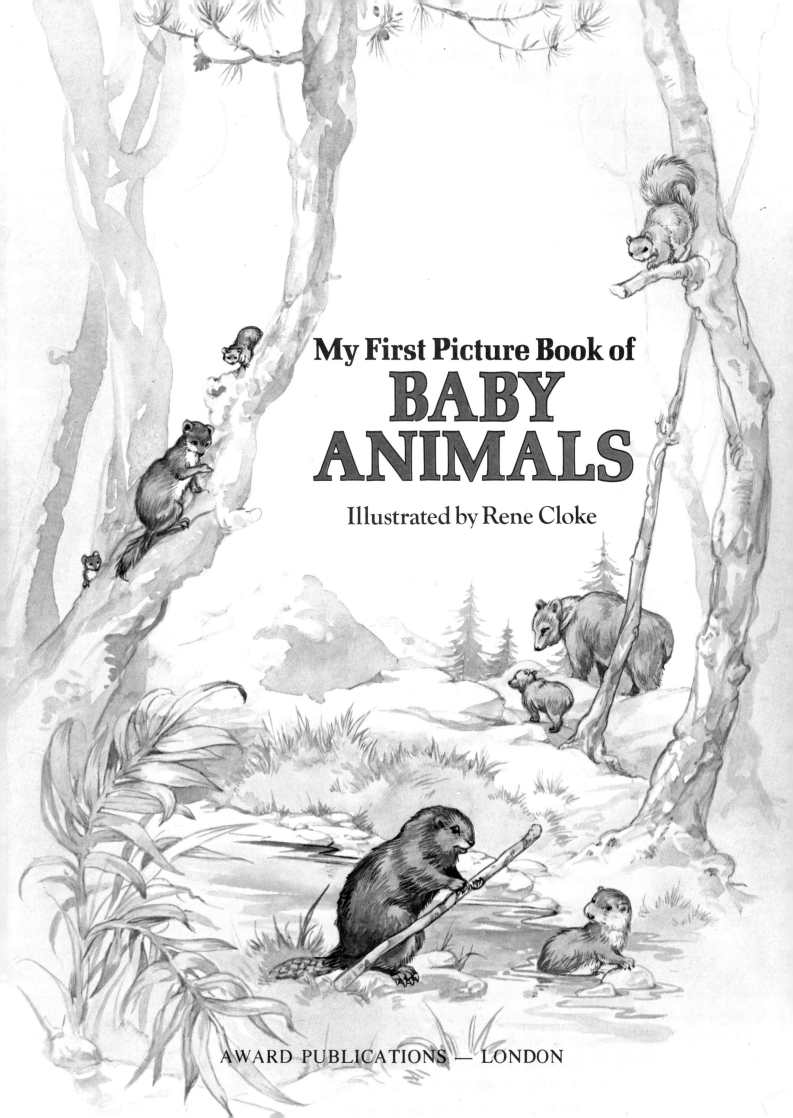

My First Picture Book of
BABY ANIMALS

Illustrated by Rene Cloke

AWARD PUBLICATIONS — LONDON

THE OTTER

The otter lives by the river or on the sea coast and its webbed feet and strong tail help it to swim well. The otter's nest is called a holt and is in the river bank, a hollow tree or cave; it feeds mostly on fish or eels.

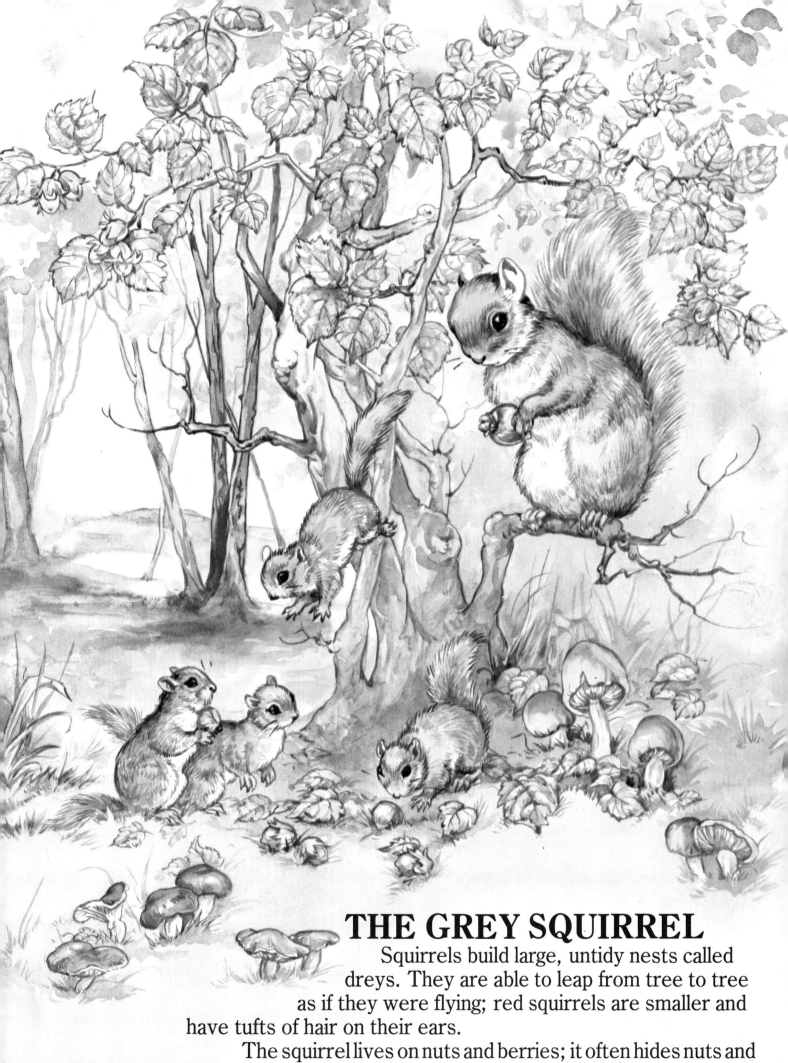

THE GREY SQUIRREL

Squirrels build large, untidy nests called dreys. They are able to leap from tree to tree as if they were flying; red squirrels are smaller and have tufts of hair on their ears.

The squirrel lives on nuts and berries; it often hides nuts and then forgets where they are buried!

THE FOX

The fox is not often seen during the day as it likes to hunt at night for rabbits, pheasants and squirrels, or chicken if a farm is near.

Its home or 'earth' is usually a burrow taken from a badger or rabbit.

The mother fox is called a vixen.

THE OPOSSUM The opossum can use its long tail like another leg when climbing. They feed on small animals as well as on fruit.

They have a clever trick of pretending to be dead to puzzle animals when being hunted.

Young opossums are carried in the mother's pouch and later on her back.

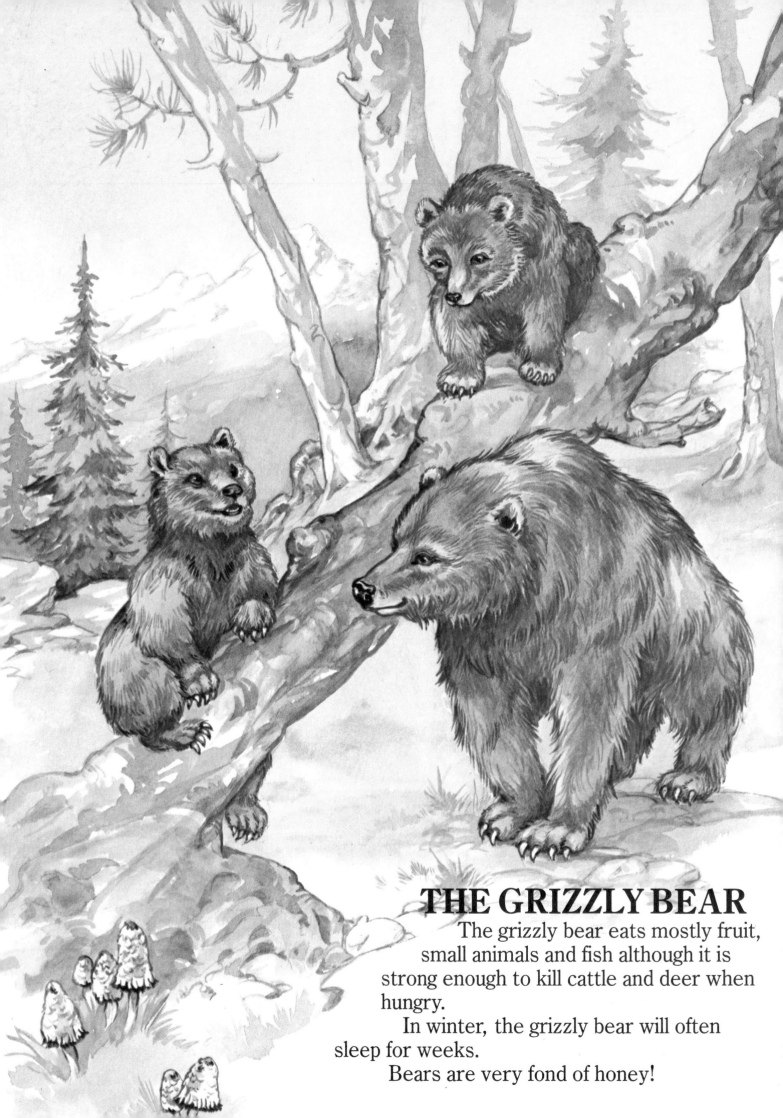

THE GRIZZLY BEAR

The grizzly bear eats mostly fruit, small animals and fish although it is strong enough to kill cattle and deer when hungry.

In winter, the grizzly bear will often sleep for weeks.

Bears are very fond of honey!

THE PRAIRIE DOG

The prairie dog lives in burrows on the prairie and eats grass.

It is more like a rat than a dog except for its bark.

THE SKUNK

Skunks make dens in rocks, in burrows and feed on insects, rats, vegetables and fruit.

They are able to squirt a smelly liquid at their enemies in defence.

The young ones are taught to follow their mother in single file.

THE BEAVER The beaver's hind feet are webbed which, with its broad flat tail, are good for swimming.

Beavers gnaw through trees to make logs. They build these across the streams so that deep pools are made to keep the entrance to their homes or 'lodges' underwater.

THE HEDGEHOG

Hedgehogs have sharp spines and are able to protect themselves by rolling into a ball.

They sleep through most of the winter in a deep bed of leaves.

The young ones are at first nearly white and have soft spines.

The hedgehog lives on snails, slugs and fruit.

THE RABBIT

Rabbits live in a warren of burrows and can do a great deal of harm to crops.

They will warn others of danger by thumping the ground with their hind feet.

THE RACCOON The raccoon lives amongst rocks or in hollow trees. It eats frogs, fish, nuts and grain, often washing the food before eating. It is able to catch fish with its paws which are almost like hands. The raccoon hunts mostly by night.

THE LYNX The lynx hunts for rabbits and birds at night and will occasionally kill a deer or sheep.

They are able to climb and swim and they use a hollow tree or sheltered cave for a home.

THE CHIPMUNK

The chipmunks are ground squirrels and live in burrows. They eat nuts, berries and grain, often storing food in their cheek pouches. Chipmunks sleep for part of the winter.

THE PORCUPINE
The porcupine is not often attacked by other animals as its quills are very sharp and painful.

They live in burrows and eat roots and fruit.

The young ones are born with short soft spines.

THE PINE MARTEN The pine marten is quite a rare animal. It nests in hollow trees or amongst rocks and will sometimes use an old crow's nest.

It feeds on mice, fish, insects and berries.

THE BADGER The badger is not
often seen except at night when it feeds on mice, young
rabbits, lizards, acorns, fruit and eggs.